D0975176

I love my Dog

I love my Dog

Georgina Harris

CICO BOOKS

LONDON NEW YORK

Dedication
To B. Pope esq., friend, wit, and renowned host

Published in 2011 by CICO Books
An imprint of Ryland Peters & Small
20–21 Jockey's Fields, London WC1R 4BW
519 Broadway, 5th Floor, New York, NY 10012

www.cicobooks.com

10 9 8 7 6 5 4 3 2 1

Text © Georgina Harris 2011
Design and illustration © CICO Books 2011

A CIP catalog record for this book is available from the Library of Congress and the British Library.

ISBN: 978 1 907563 86 7

Printed in China

Editor: Dawn Bates
Design: David Fordham
Illustration: Trina Dalziel

CONTENTS

YOUR
AMAZING
DOG

"GOD sat down for a moment
when the DOG was finished in order
to watch it... and to know that it
was good, that nothing was lacking,
that it could not have
been made better."

RAINER MARIE RILKE (1875–1926),
BOHEMIAN POET

7

"It's not the **SIZE** of the DOG in the fight, it's the **SIZE** of the fight in the DOG."

MARK TWAIN (1835–1910)

"The gift which I am sending you is called a DOG, and is in fact the most precious and valuable possession of mankind."

THEODORUS GAZA (C.1400–1475),
GREEK WRITER AND HUMANIST

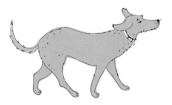

DOGS OF WAR
BRAVERY, SELF-SACRIFICE, AND SUPER-HUMAN FEATS

SAS AGENT: A long-serving member of the SAS, border collie Rob was honored for his special forces work during World War II. As an undercover agent fighting the Nazis, Rob parachuted into Italy as part of the Resistance over 20 times. He is credited with saving many agents' lives, keeping them hidden as only a DOG knows how. He was rewarded the DOG's Victoria Cross in 1945.

SEARCH AND RESCUE WARTIME HEROINE: Like her collie compatriot Rob, Sheila was also rewarded with a medal for war work. Lost in a blizzard on the Cheviot Hills in England, Christmas 1944, four US airmen were losing hope after their plane crashed and burst into flames. Part of the English rescue team, Sheila ignored the snow, sleet, and raging December winds to scour the deserted countryside. Finally, she alerted the team members to the location of the weakening crew—the airmen were saved, returned safe and warm to an English Christmas dinner, and Sheila was given the Dickin medal.

"**Y**ou think **DOGS** WILL NOT BE in heaven?

I tell you, they WILL BE there **LONG**

before any of us. "

ROBERT LOUIS STEVENSON (1850–1894)

"**I**f you pick up a starving DOG

and make him prosperous, he will not bite you;

that is the principal difference between

a DOG and a MAN."

MARK TWAIN (1835–1910)

"*H*istories are more **FULL** of examples of the fidelity of DOGS than of friends."

ALEXANDER POPE (1688 –1744)

"If you think DOGS can't count, hiding TWO DOG treats in your jacket and then handing her only ONE."

ANONYMOUS

GROUND ZERO—AND THE DOGS WHO FOUGHT TERROR

DOGS played a vital part in rescuing humans from the carnage in New York after the 9/11 bombings in 2001. New York Police Department DOGS received a special award; NYPD German Shepherd Apollo collected the Dickin Medal on behalf of his canine colleagues in the search and rescue team at Ground Zero and the Pentagon.

Apollo and his team scoured the ruins with astonishing bravery for hours, diving fearlessly into rubble and flames to search out and bring people to safety. At a special ceremony, they were commended for their "tireless courage in the service of humanity during the search and rescue operations in New York and Washington on and after 11 September 2001."

Two labradors were also honored at the ceremony; while not military personnel, Salty and Roselle saved lives too. As guide DOGS, both carefully led their blind owners down more than 70 floors of the World Trade Center to safety.

"To err is human,
to forgive, canine."

ANONYMOUS

"A DOG has one aim in life...
to bestow his heart."

J. R. ACKERLEY (1896–1967),
ENGLISH WRITER

THE PIT BULL AND THE SNAKE

With a fearsome reputation, only the families of bull terriers tend to know that it is a loyal, loving, and clever breed. None more so than Dr. Danny Fredman of Tucson, Arizona, whose young pit bull, Spike, rescued him one summer's evening. As Danny limbered up to jump into the swimming pool, Spike howled with alarm. Danny switched on the pool lights and saw a 5-ft (1.5-m) Diamondback rattlesnake coiled languorously on the water. Spike saved Danny's life—and won an animal bravery award.

PART OF THE FAMILY

"There is only one most beautiful DOG in the world, and everybody owns it."

ANONYMOUS

"**DOGS** are not our WHOLE life,

but they make

our lives WHOLE."

ROGER CARAS (1928–2001),
WILDLIFE PHOTOGRAPHER AND PRESIDENT OF THE AMERICAN SOCIETY
FOR THE PREVENTION OF CRUELTY TO ANIMALS

"The **DOG** was created specially

for children.

He is the god of *frolic*."

HENRY WARD BEECHER (1813–1887)
AMERICAN SOCIAL REFORMER AND CLERGYMAN

"When thieves come, I bark; when gallants,
I am still—
So perform both my master's
and mistress's will."

SAMUEL TAYLOR COLERIDGE (1772–1834)

"CHILDREN
are for people who can't have
DOGS."

ANONYMOUS

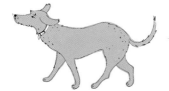

THE "ANGEL DOG"
WHO SAVED CHRISTMAS

At Christmas 2000, Iowa resident Shelby, a seven-year-old German Shepherd saved the lives of two adults and two children. Mr and Mrs Walderback and two children who were staying overnight went to bed. The children woke up feeling very sick and as Mrs Walderback rubbed their backs, she too lost consciousness. Shelby didn't hesitate—nudging and whining persistently, she revived her owner, then ran to wake Mr Walderback.

John Walderback offered Shelby an open back door, but this only distressed the big dog more—Shelby wouldn't rest until she had shepherded the couple and the children outside. At the hospital, carbon monoxide poisoning in all four humans was diagnosed. A silent, fast gas killer, the Walderbacks' home measured such high levels that death or severe injury was imminent. Joleen Walderback, the Walderbacks' daughter and owner of Shelby, concluded: "In my eyes, and in the eyes of my family, Shelby is more than a hero; she is a lifesaver, a guardian angel."

"Acquiring a **DOG** is the ONLY chance we get to choose our relations."

ANONYMOUS

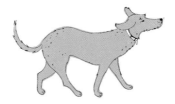

"Money will buy you a pretty good DOG, but it won't buy the wag of its tail."

HENRY WHEELER SHAW (1818–1885),
WRITING AS JOSH BILLINGS, AMERICAN HUMORIST

"I can train any **DOG** in five minutes. It's training the owner that takes **l o n g e r."**

BARBARA WOODHOUSE (1910–1988),
ENGLISH DOG TRAINER

"A DOG can show you more love with his tail in seconds than a human expresses with words **in hours."**

ANONYMOUS

"It is naught good a sleepying hound to wake."

GEOFFREY CHAUCER (C. 1343–1400), ENGLISH POET,
WHO REFERRED TO "COLLE, OUR DOGGE" IN A POEM,
THE FIRST RECORD OF A COLLIE IN THE ENGLISH LANGUAGE

"A well-behaved family DOG never begs for your lunch. He just makes you feel so bad that you won't enjoy it."

ANONYMOUS

THE WORLD'S UGLIEST DOG

Beauty is in the eye of the owner… Held in Petaluma,
California, every year, this canine "beauty" contest offers
a handsome prize of $1,000 and numerous talk show
opportunities for the lucky winner.

Sponsored by Animal Planet, the World's Ugliest Dog Contest
inspires fierce competition. DOG owners must provide proof their
DOGS are healthy, but apart from that anything goes—there is even
a pedigree category. Indeed, 2010's champion, Princess Abby, a pure-
bred chihuahua, scooped the prize. Princess Abby has a hunched and
peculiar walk due to her back legs being longer than her front legs, only
one eye, and mismatched ears. She saw off 25 opponents. Owner
Francis explained that the Humane Society rescued Abby, starving
and covered in fleas, barely six months before she won the competition.
And for Francis, visiting the pound at Clear Lake, it was love at first sight.

YOUR BEST FRIEND

"It is scarcely possible to doubt that the love of man has become instinctive in the DOG."

CHARLES DARWIN (1809–1882)

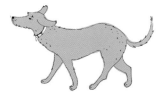

"No man can be
condemned for owning a DOG.
As long as he has a DOG, he has a friend;
and the POORER he gets, the BETTER
friend he has."

WILL ROGERS (1879–1935),
AMERICAN WRITER AND HUMORIST

"My little DOG—a heartbeat at my feet."

EDITH WHARTON (1862–1937)

FAITHFUL DOGS:
THE DOG THAT DUELLED FOR HIS MASTER

More than just a cliche, the family DOG's loyalty to family
and friends has been proven over centuries. In the 15th
century at the court of French King Charles V, the courtier
Aubry De Montdidier was found murdered in the palace's
forest. His killer remained at large until Dragon, Aubry's
sweet-natured greyhound, flew on the man, in public. The
King sensed trouble—and ordered the pair to trial by combat.

The greyhound, unarmed, fought the cudgel-
bearing assailant, and won the duel. The
murderer was hanged, and Dragon was
immortalized in the book *The Dog of Montargis*.

"To a man, the **greatest** blessing is

individual liberty.

To a DOG, it is the last word in **despair**."

WILLIAM LYON PHILLIPS (1865–1943)

"Aim to be as fine a person
as your DOG thinks you are."

ANONYMOUS

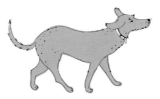

"It's no coincidence that man's best friend cannot talk."

"One reason your DOG is such a comfort when you're gloomy is that he NEVER asks why."

"To his DOG,

every man is NAPOLEON,

hence the constant popularity of DOGS."

ALDOUS HUXLEY (1894–1963)

"WE long for an affection altogether

ignorant of our faults.

Heaven has accorded this to us

in the uncritical canine attachment."

GEORGE ELIOT (1819–1880)

PRESIDENTS AND POOCHES

What really matters to the most powerful

people on the planet (and their human owners)?

As the mightiest man in the land,

the US president has always used his august

position to make pronouncements on life's most vital matters.

So it's no surprise that several of America's finest leaders have

declared the importance of the humble hound:

> **"I care not for a man's religion whose DOG and cat
> are not the better for it."**

ABRAHAM LINCOLN (1809 –1865), 16TH PRESIDENT OF THE UNITED STATES—
OWNER OF FIDO, ONE OF THE FIRST DOGS EVER PHOTOGRAPHED

"If a DOG will not come to you after having looked you in the face, you should go home and examine your conscience."

WOODROW WILSON (1856–1924), 28TH PRESIDENT OF THE UNITED STATES —
NOT A DOG OWNER WHILE IN OFFICE, BUT SHOOK THE PAW OF
SPYCATCHER STUBBY, A BULL TERRIER

"Any man who does not like DOGS and want them about does not deserve to be in the White House."

CALVIN COOLIDGE (1872–1933), 30TH PRESIDENT OF THE UNITED STATES —
OWNED 12 DOGS, RANGING FROM COLLIES TO CHOW CHOWS AND A POLICE DOG

"Children and DOGS are as necessary to the welfare of the country as Wall Street and the railroads."

HARRY S. TRUMAN (1884–1972), 33RD PRESIDENT OF THE UNITED STATES—
VERY FOND OF HIS MONGREL, FELLER, AND MIKE, HIS IRISH SETTER

"Buy a pup and your money will buy Love U^NF_LI^NC^H_IN^G that cannot lie."

RUDYARD KIPLING (1865–1936)

"No one truly appreciates the fascination of your conversation like your DOG."

ANONYMOUS

"We allow our FRIENDS
into our company,
but we allow our DOGS into our solitude."

ANONYMOUS

"The GREAT pleasure of a DOG
is that you may
MAKE A FOOL OUT OF YOURSELF
with him, and not only will he not scold you,
but he will MAKE A FOOL OUT OF HIMSELF too."

SAMUEL BUTLER(1835–1902),
ENGLISH NOVELIST

"They never TALK ABOUT THEMSELVES
but listen to you
while you TALK ABOUT YOURSELF,
and keep up an appearance
of being interested in the conversation."

JEROME K. JEROME (1859 –1927)

"If you eliminate smoking and gambling,
you will be amazed to find
that almost ALL an Englishman's pleasures
CAN BE, and MOSTLY ARE,
shared by his DOG."

GEORGE BERNARD SHAW (1856–1950),
IRISH PLAYWRIGHT AND PHILOSOPHER

"*H*e cannot be a **gentleman** which loveth not a DOG."

"A DOG is the only creature
who will love you more than
he loves himself."

"Recollect that the ALMIGHTY,
who gave the DOG to be companion of our pleasures
and our toils, hath invested him with a nature
noble and incapable of deceit."

SIR WALTER SCOTT (1771–1832),
SCOTTISH NOVELIST AND POET IN THE TALISMAN

"DOGS love their friends and bite their enemies,
quite unlike people, who are incapable of pure love
and always have to mix love and hate."

SIGMUND FREUD (1856–1939)—
FREUD'S FAVORITE DOG WAS JO-FI, A CHOW CHOW WHO OFTEN SAT IN ON THERAPY
SESSIONS AND CALMED AND RELAXED FREUD'S PATIENTS

Picture Credits

Copyright © Cico Books
Mark Lohman p1, pp38–39, pp44-45; Mark Scott 41; Keith Scott Morton p48; Edina van der Wyck p5 above right, pp12-13, 38-39

Copyright © Ryland Peters & Small
Lina Ikse Bergman p5 below right, p55; Christopher Drake pp56-57; Chris Everard p5 left, p27, p59; Tom Leighton p46; Chris Tubbs p18; Jo Tyler pp2-3; Andrew Wood p60; Polly Wreford p64

Used under licence from ShutterStock, 2011
Tpp 6-7 lexan; p 9 WilleeCole; p10 gbphoto1; p14 Emily Veinglory; p17 Tatagatta; p21 Rosamund Parkinson; pp22-23 FotoJagodka; p25 Anna Utekhina; p28 argo74; p31 Raywoo; p32 FeatherFantasy; p35 cluckva; p36 Aaron Amat; p42 Svetlana Valoueva; p51 mikeledray; p52 baronb; p63 Joop Snijder jr.

Dog breeds: p1 Yorkshire Terrier; p2 Jack Russell; p5 Cocker Spaniel (left); Lhasa Apso (above right); Jack Russell (below right); p7 Dalmatian; p9 English Bulldog; p10 and p14 Border Collie; p13 Lhasa Apso; p17 German Shepherd; p18 Labrador; p20 American Blue Pit Bull; p22 Papillon; p25: Miniature poodle; p27: Cocker Spaniel; p28 German Shepherd; p31 Golden Retriever; p32 Jack Russell; p35 Labrador; p36 Chihuahua; p38 Poodle; p41 Breed unknown; p42 Greyhound; p45 Breed unknown; p46 Jack Russell; P48 Australian Collie; p50 Bichon Frieze; p52 Chow Chow; p55 Jack Russell; p56 King Charles Spaniel; p59 Labrador; p60 Irish Wolfhound; p63 Golden Retriever; p64 Jack Russell

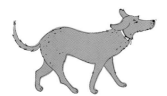